PARROT WITH TOURETTE'S

Poems By

RICHARD STEVENSON

National Library of Canada Cataloguing in Publication

Stevenson, Richard, 1952-
   Parrot with Tourette's / Richard Stevenson.

(Palm poets series)
ISBN 0-88753-398-1

   I. Title. II. Series.

PS8587.T479P37 2004   C811'.54   C2004-901868-X

The Palm Poets Series is published by Black Moss Press at 2450 Byng Road, Windsor, Ontario N8W 3E8. Black Moss books are distributed in Canada and the U.S. by Firefly Books, 3680 Victoria Park Ave., Willowdale, Ont. Canada. All orders should be directed there.

Black Moss would like to acknowledge the generous support of the Canada Council and the Ontario Arts Council for its publishing program.

I

Unemployed in Shangri-La

Canada Geese Nesting Site

And now, ladies and gentlemen,
direct from Lake Tahoe,
here on the back swing
of their sell-out western tour –
for one spring only! —
the quintessentially Canadian,
the very excellent,
the sleek and radiant
father and mother act
you've been waiting
all winter to see –
the Canada Geese!

Honk! Honk! Yes, thank you, thank you.
Wonderful to be here
in your fair city of – what? —
Honk! Honk! Lethbridge is it? Yes.
Well, wonderful, just wonderful.
Honk! And nice to see

so many of you fine folks
bundled up, walking past
our little island community — honk! —
with dogs and kids in tow – honk! —
on roller blades and jogging.
Honk! Honk! We thought
we'd share that lovely spring ritual –
honk! — that very goosey business
of goosing the missus and – honk! —
procreating for you all – honk! —
and shell out a few goslings
for this – honk! honk! — gaggle of groupies
you might say. Honk! Honk! Harrggghhhh –
Ahhh – Sorry, a little indigestion.
Didn't mean to foul the nestin'.
Honk! Honk! Well, you know –
loose as a goose, as they say –
even the great Caruso
got to clear his throat
before he sang. Har! Har! Honk!
Honk! Honk! Honk! Honk!

Anecdote of the Glass

(for Eddie Fitzgerald)

You know the one –
the conundrum of whether
a glass is half-full
or half-empty that
smart aleck teachers
and philosophy profs
like to tease kids with.

Well, it's simple really –
and contrary to the so-called
wisdom of the dim
teacher who told me
there was no logical
solution to the problem,
there is one. A simple one.

It's a question, right?
And for every question
there is an answer,

7

whether we know it or not.
For this one, it depends
whether you are emptying
the glass or filling it.

If you are filling it,
the glass of half-full;
if you are emptying it,
it's half-empty. Simple.
Now, you want a metaphor?
It's about the container,
not what's in it, obviously.

Communication Gaff

Solicitous job seeker
to the blonde missus entreats,
"I'd like to connect
your acquaintance, madam."
Husband, looking on,
smirks and replies,
" I bet you would."

(Maiduguri, Nigeria)

Translation Please

Bature, come!
You go take dis magani
E be good for jiggy jig.
You go last long time.
You go make am babies plenty.
I tink you sabe, ba?

My wife isn't pregnant.
Can't I get it up?
Take this … in memory of what?
What is the sound
of one kid kicking?

(Maiduguri, Nigeria)

Two Mormon Missionaries

Hardly ancient mariners
in their white shirts and ties,
though they may stoppeth one in ten.

They work the strip between
golf links and Japanese Garden,
catch joggers, locals walking their dogs.

Chain Link Tanka

(For The Jerk Next Door)

Our neighbour hates cats,
wants ours off his property
or else he'll bait traps -
as if cats understand yards,
the terrible leash of words.

I tell him if he
so much as touches our cats,
I'll beat him senseless,
and we bark at each other
over the back fence.

The guy's an asshole
surrounded by cat lovers.
Thinks ours are the ones
responsible for the shit
he finds in his flower beds.

Maybe I should coil
a mainspring on his front lawn,
gather our dog's shit,
fling it on his roof one night,
tell him it's condor droppings.

Unemployed in Shangri-La

1. When You're Single

When you're single
it's easy to be cavalier
even blazé about these things:

To be unemployed is to be free,
to be granted an unexpected holiday,
or stay of execution.

On Judge Place in Victoria, B.C. –
city of newlyweds and nearly deads –
my university friends sleep in,

raise noses from the basement burrows
of their parents' homes
only when the mailman brings their pogey.

Mail slots open and close:
mouths of ungainly nestlings
craning for the early worm.

Doors open and close in unison
like the startled lids of groundhogs
reluctant to see their shadows.

Even the ducks paddle about the winter ponds
and fart in shallow water with impunity.
A little flatus propels them into a state of grace.

When you're single, it is nothing to eat air.
You can pretend to be a duck and glide downstream.
Or you can rise on the elastic ebullience of ideas.

Ideas come cheap and no one listens to them
because they have no face value or currency
among those burdened with work.

They can't be translated into fuel
or food or shelter or power or faith.
They have no bellies to fill.

2. Life is a Sentence

Consider the athletic young twenty-year-olds
who gather like a gaggle of Canada geese
each winter at the Banff Springs Hotel:

each boasts bulging biceps and a tan,
stands tall in snow-white T-shirt
emblazoned with the logo of the U.I.C. ski team.

For such a person, unemployment is but a dream.
A brief respite from the endless round
of McJobs he'd as soon wake from as work at.

Life is a sentence
ending only with the preposition *to:*
a vector of some vague promissory note

propelling him from one envisioned future
to another. He is unemployed in Shangri-La,
and has a nest egg he can hatch.

3. The U.I.C. Case Load Worker's Position

For the government worker at C.E.C.
the unemployed are clients in a burgeoning case load;
they must be eliminated or expunged.

Workers are cattle to be herded by velvet ropes
into some magic corral. They must take numbers,
wait for the auctioneer to sort them into lots.

Some workers are diseased by their lack of work.
Case workers can see this, and so approach
clients with gloves and surgical masks.

They would quarantine such clients
with small infusions of cash
and thereby contain the clients' contagion.

Some workers are already sandwich meat;
lips and fingernails and bone ground up
and compressed into thin sheets of paper.

They fit neatly between the white bread slices
of files and perfect consumer incisors of
U.I.C. workers' orthodontured teeth.

If these clients are not wearing
sandwich boards, they are already eaten
or are busy consuming themselves with guilt.

4. The U.I.C. Clients' Position

All of us on the consumer side of the counter
have bemused looks on our faces. We wonder
how it is a mere counter – wood and arborite –
can give U.I.C. workers such sharp teeth?

Do they gnaw on the arborite and plywood
like diligent little Canadian beavers?
Is it absolutely necessary –
to prevent involuntary malocclusion,
they being so perpetually long in the tooth?
Do their teeth not stop growing
unless they constantly wear them down
by chewing on the gross national product?

Surely, we are the reason they can brush
their teeth after every meal, after all.
We are the milk bone biscuits they chew
and spit out every day. The raw leather
of falsified statistics they whet their teeth on.
Is it puppy love that makes them maul us so?
We would gladly work, even trade sides
were it not for the fact that
Good-one-side lumber gives us
such awful indigestion.

5. Snakes and Ladders – or Monopoly?

Sometimes this seems like a Monopoly game:
if you do not pass go (i.e. work a certain
minimum number of insurable weeks),
you do not collect two hundred dollars.

You always seem to get laid off
before you've logged enough time,
but each and every week you've worked
the pogey payment comes off your cheque.

Or maybe it's like Snakes and Ladders:
Everything's going great: you've enjoyed
a long period of prosperity, climbed
a lot of rungs when —

W
 O
  O
   O
    O
    S
     H
      H
       !

— you hit a snake and backslide
to your starting position.

You've got a choice: hoard your doubloons
or ride a lot of snakes to the grave.

Either way, come claim time,
there will be a lot of forms to fill out,
a lot of flip charts and game pieces to move.

I wonder: does God work for Milton Bradley?
What's his percentage in all of this?

17

John

With some kids it begins
with breaking bobbing bottles,
hitting tin cans on a fence.

They discover slingshots,
arrows, air rifles,
move on to pot frogs.

But for John, killing was not
a matter of getting off a good shot.
A frog didn't squirm quite like a dog.

One time he put on garden gloves
to hold down the neighbour's cat
long enough to get a firecracker up its ass.

His pupils grew as black and deep
as the well he drowned his puppies in.
No one saw to their bottom then.

He tore a kid's ear off once too, they say.
Pinned him down and beat his head with a rock.
Some say he found an outlet: now he's a cop.

Relief Janitor's Lament

You get used to cleaning up girls washrooms,
and fewer "ladies" leave "powder rooms"
than come in to take a powder, I can tell you.

They forget to flush as often as the boys do,
write graffiti on the cubicle walls,
and plug up the sinks with paper towels.

Small wonder they call these biffies bogs:
you need a pair of hip waders
as well as a snake to unplug the drains —

and, yes, the girls play the games the boys do:
they write you notes: who to call for a good time,
and what she'll do to you when you do.

You develop a prurient interest in these things.
They're like the soaps: you scrub off the walls,
but stay tuned to the next in-stall-ment.

Today the female lead's exit bit's writ large,
emblazoned in tampon script across the mirror:
"Put your hairy snake in my hairy hole."

I'm more amazed at the reference to pubic hair
than I am by the lewdness of the message
or the crude cool medium, as McLuhan would put it.

This school only goes to grade six!
Where do you learn stuff like this?
I want to write, but, instead, wipe it off.

I mean, most girls this age
try to hide the evidence of the way
nature has betrayed them. They blush and flush.

This girl's writing bloody eye-ku
that cannot be erased! Whose daughter is she,
whose girl that she should express such rage,

such brazen defiance of all the dirty Ernies
of this world who would sit her on their laps
or look for reflections in her patent leather shoes?

Is it a telling detail that she used
the tampon receptacle for an ash tray?
What stub burns to the quick of her heart?

What fish did she think to play out
by feeding toilet paper straight off the spool
into the loo? Who did she expect to land it?

Me! Without hip waders, a gaff, or a net —
and now without even a fine reticulated net of emotions
to catch her falling. Sweetheart, what happened to you?

Supply Teacher / Relief Janitor

It starts with a simple phone call:
"Joe's slipped a disk; we need
a relief janitor for three weeks at least.
Are you free? Can you do his shift?"

The arithmetic's easy: a cheque
minus rent, groceries, pogey.
Sure, I say. Four to midnight?
No problem. Days I can sit by the phone.

Then the call comes from the same school:
Can you teach? English, Social Studies —
Grade twelve no less: another two weeks.
I'm elated; think this will be fun:

Sport jacket, slacks, briefcase —
a chance to make professional contacts
in the staff room by day;
get the real poop from the broom boys at night.

And so it goes too, until I start
feeling like Clark Kent, furtive, on edge,
always looking for a closet, phone booth
from which to emerge in Adidas and jeans.

The thing is, I have the game plan reversed.
I start out with the broom, so this guy
begins to patronize me about the way
he wants his room cleaned every night.

He speaks slowly, enunciates every syllable
as though he were talking to a five-year old boy,
so, slack-jawed, I practically slobber on him
and oblige him with my best spaniel act.

Listen, bub, if your asshole were as squeaky clean
as your room at the end of each shift,
I wouldn't be picking up your washers
everywhere I walk, I want to say,

but no: I just nod and grin to myself.
Tomorrow I'll see him in the staff room,
watch his jaw drop. He's got a mouth
like a toilet lid, as my Mom'd say:

always catching flies. A regular mobius strip
for a tongue too. And tomorrow his eyes
will look like his classroom window ledge
before I start vacuuming up their flies.

For Eddie Fitzgerald,
On The Leg Home

Eddie Frances Fitzgerald's
logged 122,00 miles –
beat the Guiness Book record
for longest trip by bicycle.

A regular ancient mariner
who hath the beguiling manner,
baby blues, and craggy face
to stoppeth me – and a few
other pigeons in the park today.

He layeth the boney finger on me –
not to waylay me with some
sad tale of an albatross
that bought the farm on his account –

he's got a stack of xeroxed
newspaper articles to do that nicely –
but to help pay for another meal,
a new seat for Maggie,
his fourteenth bike, his lady love.

He's lost fifty pounds trying
to outrun the grief he feels
after losing his wife of thirty years
to leukemia, and tells me
he hasn't so much run from life
as run pell mell into it.

Has run into too many people
with no feet to be crying
because he has no shoes.
Doesn't need a stainless steel
proctol bike pole up the ass
while he rides into the next day's molecules.

Has only 8,000 miles to go
to get home, where three pensions,
two kids, and five grandchildren
line up like gew gaws on a windowsill.
They don't get it, of course.

Never did. Not for any of the
fourteen years he's been on the road.
But there's a book deal to think of,
and his son's a C.P.A. who has
made sure he won't have to
bend over to touch his toes
to find out where that wild goose goes.

So he keeps riding. Sometimes 100 miles,
most often, 25 or 30 a day –
and keeps his eyes open for an Irish
pub or quiet glade to have
a little nip before shoving off again.

And regales me with three –
then another buck's worth of wit
until I wander off to walk my dog
on the paved path around a lake
the perimeter of which seems shorter today.

Arf, arf, I want to say,
the dog dragging me toward
a gaggle of geese – here
"for our viewing pleasure,"
according to the park sign
that warns us not to feed them.
And who hath the shorter lease –
or should I say leash –
on this domestic life?

How bad do I look? Eddie wants to know,
asking the same question of all wedding guests,
laughing at his own wizened
jack-o-lantern visage in the mirror,
an old friend's tested and testy reply,
"Good enough for an open coffin when you die."

Parrot With Tourette's

— for Robert Sward

Q. What does a 500-pound parrot say?
A. Polly want a cracker – right fuckin' now!

It's not the parrot's fault, really –
He's just a mimic, after all –
merely repeats whatever vocalizations
he hears or finds easy to replicate
in his wisecracking slobovian squawk.

It's the boarder with Tourette's syndrome
who breaks into choice one-syllable
Anglo Saxon words, and curses
like an involuntary trooper when he's nervous.

He's nervous a lot. But imagine
how useful such a fine-feathered
Mac of a macaw could be. The vicar
stays too long for tea, say –

is going on about sin and redemption,
spitting his venomous spleen
all over the dollies and fine bone china.
Lift the cover from the cage and – presto! –

his stiff collar's scorched in an instant;
his arched caterpillar brows are singed, baby!
He'd uncross his legs on the Hepplewhite in a hurry,
scurry for the door like some rodent

out of Beatrix Potter, Adam's apple
bobbing as he sputtered and spluttered
his easily borrowed outrage. A handsome tool
for the quick removal of any household prude!

Fuck you and the horse you rode in on!
Fuck me blue, baby! Roll me over
in the clover. Do it again. Rock my body
til I ain't got a bone! Is that a gun …?

Squ-aw-awk! Squ-aw-awk!
Polly want a cracker, motherfucker!
Bring on the grub, bub! And while you're at it,
How's about lettin' that scarlet bitch in here?

I wanna bump uglies; fuck bumpin' gums!
Squ-aw-awk! Squ-aw-awk!
Get down, baby! Ooo, ooo … Granny cut your toenails;
you're rippin' up the !@#$% sheets!*

Such high vocalic runs of grace!
In your face, baby! Imagine teaching him
limericks. You could charge the neighbours
for nightly recitations! Take him to the pub!

Have him curse for your supper 'n' suds!
Let him roll his r's in front of the heat registers,
or give him a megaphone to do his thing
whenever holy rollers roll up to the door!

Take that! Rat-a-tat-tat! Ol' Edward G.
couldn't lay waste to the coppers of any B
gangster flick with half as much aplomb
if he had two choppers spittin' and smokin'!

You gotta admit, the Polly wanna cracker gag
is stale, baby, stale! Better this Oscar Brand
rag while you tickle the ivories of that baby grand.
Better a falsetto stream of alliterative abuse

than hearing yourself parrot ol' rhetoric
as you pout and croon in front of
some gilded cage, expecting his pupils to dilate.
Polly can't fuckin' relate. It's late, baby, late!

The Embolism

(for Susan)

Your fifth dive,
surfacing from sixty feet.
You pull the J-valve
like a cork from a bottle.

I want to say champagne
bubbles are released,
the surface is
a hogshead of real fire,

the jinn in that cylinder
so cramped, so desirous
of its own freedom
you can only follow it,

but the world is indeed
too much with us,
and slaps you in the face
instead of on the bottom.

We too, sheath-wet
in our second skins,
stand upon the shore
like acolytes to greet you,

only the mist
from our masks
is not blue smoke
dispensed from censers,

and can keep nothing at bay
for all the susurration
of waves saying shh, shhh,
it's all right, it's O.K.

And nothing is
and nothing will be again
for the man laying prone
flippers splayed

is no clown or seal
waiting his turn to jump
from drum to drum
through imagined flames,

and no Charlie Chaplin
whose pratfalls are endearing,
so safely taken in transfusion
up a black chord from a wall.

His fall from grace
the result of using his reserve
to descend rather than ascend,
of not following his jinn into space.

The kelp offshore writhe:
a den of snakes he should have
climbed over and not tried
to swim under with so little air.

Now sky pinches, a round
rubber seal that holds
your ruptured world at bay.
We bow heads and pray.

We must all look like fish
pressed against the glass
the thickness of two skins away,
our words so many bubbles rising…

31

But to what surface now?
There is no way we can get
the jinn back in the bottle,
let alone this man's burst lungs.

Waves lap against the shore,
each and every one of them
a draw sheet pulled taut
over your father's face.

32

II
Body English

The Slice

On the top lawn, next to the garage,
Garth prepares to tee off, pauses
while my sister, Donna, looks on.

He has a plan. One he and David
have concocted, one my brother
and I were not near enough to hear.

I imagine the words, hard and round,
contained a rubber bladder of vitriol
wound in miles of elastic so they would

fly as far as a golf ball does
when a man addresses it with a club.
Words like the first golf ball my brother

sliced open with an axe on a stump,
that bear the scars we call smiles,
sliced clean through the casing.

Time was we found such balls in bushes,
stepped on them in gumboots in ditches.
Put chalk in the cracks, painted them over.

Sold them to unsuspecting golfers,
who sliced or hooked them back
into our pockets. Fondled them like bird eggs.

We even kept them in egg cartons.
Saved the "crocks" to tee off toward
the recluse neighbours' high windows.

That was the plan. Not now.
Now Garth has a better idea. Swings hard
to open a smile in my sister's temple.

And blood takes flight: surprise chevron
on a blackbird's wing. Flashes once
as a new truth flees the rushes of youth

and a boy gets too close to a nest.
These words, like the untouched ball
sit high and hard on a tee inside me.

Await the steel shank, the hard, flat
surface of a five-iron to smack them
again and again back into the bush.

Body Sculpture

(for Donna)

Body sculpture is how my
sister describes the process —
as if a woman might become
the smithy of her soul
by reclaiming the image of her flesh.

And to that end, she lifts, pulls,
shoves apposing muscles;
builds, tones, defines,
tans existing body mass.
Teases, shaves, waxes away unwanted hair.

Praxiteles, Michelangelo, Rodin —
all men, sculpting men's
and women's bodies and minds
after ideals patriarchies defined —
not even the aerodynamics of Mr. Brassiere
could offer more for the light to revere.

For the glare of the kliegs,
even the interrogation of a cannon spot
cannot belie evidence of what the regimen
of work, amino acids, hormones,
diuretics and oil have done.

She's never tried to achieve this
degree or kind of power over men
with clothes or make-up,
suddenly finds herself sexy as she
strides through the turnstile of eyes.

And why shouldn't she strut her stuff?
It is only men who want women
totally pneumatic and soft, so that
they might pump themselves up
by pumping iron and air.

Men are born with a mirror before them
and need no balance beam
but the hand-held purchase
their eyes make of place.
Women provide negative space.

The Golden Spike Award

(for Donna)

Of all the body building trophies my sister has won —
and she has a closet full she'd as soon melt down
or trade for cash, if they weren't plastic —
this is the one she chooses to enshrine:
an ordinary six-inch spike painted gold
and mounted in a wood-lathed four-by-four base.
A joke, born of a chance remark
an acquaintance once made,
presented by my brother with mock pomp
in some circumstance we've all since forgotten.
The Golden Spike Award
from the Academy of Soft-Hearted Fools
whose strength and singularity of purpose
are not up to yours. To the new you: beautiful woman
"with an ass that could pull nails out of walls."
All our walls. With Love, The Dumb Bell Crew.

39

Dorfy II

(for Marika)

We gather her hair in pigtails,
accede to her demands for a cotton dress
and black patent leather shoes.

The wicker basket was her idea from the start —
as was the sandy, plush toy spaniel
she dubs "Todo" and puts in the basket.

The rest is a whirligig of joy —
tripping the light fantastic
down an imaginary yellow brick road.

Thankfully, she's "Dorfy," and not the cyclone.
Our screen door stays intact, and, so far, the house
continues to hunker on its foundation.

For that, and the conspicuous lack
of thousands of Munchkins, we are grateful.
Agree to fend off the lions and tigers and bears.

We watch with joy as Dorfy makes her way
to her Emerald City, blissfully skipping
through the dark wood, "Off to see a wizard."

Will she get there, we wonder.
Will she always be able to follow her bliss?
Questions merely deadfalls across her path.

She sidesteps them easily,
leaves her babyhood with the cherubic pink
child molt asleep with her "uggies" —

Albert, the hand-puppet Albertasaurus,
Spot Uggy, Bradley Brontosaurus and friends —
the indispensable blanket she calls her "bunt,"

as if these were merely characters, props
left over from some other movie set
stricken, carted back to Kansas

or wherever the cyclone in her head
set them down after so many witches
and flying monkeys carted off her day.

For this is a sequel. Call it Dorfy II:
the world is soon playing
at a theatre near you.

Kick Boxing With My Daughter

(for Marika)

Jab! Cross! Jab!
The instructor barks,
and we biff, bop, box
our serious reflections
with equal vehemence;

right, left, right –
advance toward the mirror.
Even Frankenstein's monster
would be hard pressed
to stagger with less grace –

but – hey! — we're learning –
and – what the hell –
a co-ed pummeling is
something our Doppelgangers
can definitely take –

especially if it means
I lose a little weight
and get to wink at
my daughter in her
"Canadian Girls Kick Ass" T-shirt.

She's got twelve-year old
adolescent demons to acquaint
with the Queensbury rules;
I've got this grey-haired fool
whose rueful grin needs removal.

So we dance – together –
twice a week, though
bones and muscles I didn't
know I had ache to
remind me of my middle age.

Practice muyi thai, axe,
and roundhouse kicks,
pivot on rusty hinges
stiffer than the turnstile
of all these knowing eyes;

are greeted cheerfully nonetheless –
twice a week. Oh would that
the turnstile would slap
my ass like a wet towel –
on the way out.

I would not flinch
or yelp like these young pups,
would not reach for my puffer,
but would grin at the geezer
twisting the towel in the mirror,

and would vault
right over the counter
into the next life,
ready to spar with the devil –
or God himself in his tear-off togs.

I'd skip forever and never
get the rope caught between
my toes. Do figure eights
to keep my daughter
jumping the same rope.

Push-ups, burpees, crunchies,
weights – baby, keep pumpin!
I'd say – and hold the moon
like a limbo stick at my fevered brow
forever for her to shimmy under.

For it's worth it! If not for
the washboard tummy
or heavy metal thunder
of hard body intelligence,
then just to hop one more fence.

Jab! Cross! Jab!
We take it on the chin,
shins, hips, ribs – together –
the purple pleura of the sky
engorged once more in a beautiful bruise.

Growing a Beard

One can become obsessed with hair —
in growing a beard for example —
this experiment:
Jekyll and Hyde transformation,
Darwin's theory in reverse:
me Tarzan, you Jane.

I've got six weeks
to pull the masquerade off.
A simple task one would think:
the rules clear-cut, defined:
leave the razor where it lies,
abandon the sacramental solutions
of shaving cream and aftershave,

return in afternoon shadow
when I've disappeared behind
a wall of mumbles and broken sticks:
a new anthropoid, silhouette stretching
a kind of ground cover across the miles,
disguising a low tide in the genetic pool.

I gaze into the mirror and wonder
what school of fish Narcissus
might have seen had he been
as furry as his ancestors, less given
to navel-gazing or solipsistic ellipses.

Growing a beard is growing out of place.
That much said, I can let
my doppelganger hang by five
fingers from the trees. Let the breeze
lick my furry jowls like a new-born pup.
Looking in the mirror is looking up.

47

Vasectomy

The decision was simple enough.
Sex isn't some funny uncle from Desmoines
who talks your ear off about plumbing
fixtures and valves, or harrumphs and egads
his way through hot tips of insider trading
while he puffs away at his dime store cigar.

You can't console it with a back rub
or dusty old tin of Copenhagen snuff —
even if it promises you candy
or a shiny new silver dollar
for going to the store for it.

You are not a piggy bank
and it can't fill you up that way.
Nor is your body a parking meter
that can take pills like endless
rolls of quarters, and always be there
when you want to go out dancing.

We cannot expect lightning bolts from heaven
to light up the main circuit panel
then travel down the line
to some copper key kited high
inside your uterus either —
not without blasting the tree
to its very roots.

Love is not a shooting gallery.
There is no one to yell "pull,"
no guarantee every clay pigeon
will be hit by a perfect bullet,
even now when I plan on shooting blanks.
The target is not something you hit or miss.

You were not made from Adam's
or anyone's rib, as the fused halves
of my glans, the line up
the shaft of my penis show.

49

The decision was simple,
something we could even be glib about:
it's easier to work on outside plumbing
than chase a knotted bit of cloth
with a snake throughout your pipes.

Just as we turn off the inside taps
so the water in the outside faucets won't freeze
and burst the pipes behind the drywall,
this little precaution with my spigot
may steal a little juice from Peter
so we might afford to pay Paul.

Or say we are tending our garden, love —
pruning suckers from last year's roses
so they continue to bloom with promises.
Though our children grow apace,
we can find the garden again.
We need only tag a branch,
to find our old initials
still growing with the tree.

50

My Ears

Pinnae, to be specific: the funnels
that channel sound through the ear canal
past hammers, anvils, and stirrups to cochlea.

Not particularly big or flappy,
though I was a while growing
into mine, judging from family photos.

Might have given Bing Crosby or even
Prince Charles a run for their money
in my youth. Might have sailed on skates –

no thanks to the geek buzz cuts
that the old man and local barber favoured
until the block cut came around.

Is it any wonder I became a hippie
and chose to hide them for a couple
of decades, was never a Mickey Mouse fan?

51

Then on a whim in my forties
I punctured one for a stud –
wrong ear as it turned out —

the gay side, though it doesn't
much matter these days
that I soon had the other done.

One ring in my left ear –
above a long scar where the last
in a series of doctors operated –

partial parotidectomy – to get at,
hunt down, and remove a long tube-like
branchial cleft cyst. Had to inject dye

to see where the damn branches grew –
a virtual tree growing down
the outside of my throat, as it turned out!

And now the hollow created by refusal
of squamous and ear canal tissue
to fuse. Gets infected, fills up with

dead white blood cells. At least the doc
put the ear back in the right place,
opposite its twin, a pair of parentheses ... .

It's the vacant space between
the two eyes with signs "To Let"
he might have worried about,

and I can still scuba dive –
though I lost the bet over being
able to get into my wet suit,

not on account of my gut,
but on account of a bigger nose!
At least my glasses hang straight!

53

My Nose

Not particularly huge,
but bony and avuncular;
plugged and afunctional
when not Otrivin-primed,
poked, prodded, preened,
blown amelodiously
most saxophoniously loud;
my little badass huzzah
whazzat ah choosey snout
of a snoz! Say it loud
and say it proud!
Wha-za –wha-za – whazzat
If it snot white boy funk?!

54

My Calves

Best feature – not counting my
somewhat functional brain.

Big, heavy, muscular – with cleft
down the middle when I
stand on my toes.

A weightlifter's calves, though
any cleaning and jerking or squats I do
is inevitably at the end of a broom.

My more athletic friends all say
body builders would kill to have 'em.
I was born lucky somehow.

I don't know. I tend to think
the reason I have thick calves
is because I'm so short –

the muscles of my legs kind of
got caught in a permanent crouch
or bunched up when there was nowhere to reach

for. The bones were too short
for the muscles to stretch out is all.
But I say my legs are perfect:

they reach all the way
from my squat little torso
to the ground, and hold me up just fine!

56

My Anus

Twitchy asterisk: always has
something to say, even if
it's only mastered sibilants
and the anal fricative – fff,
sss – and the odd vowel/consonant
combination: fffrrr – aaa – ppp!

Particularly vocal if there's
a reason not to be, it seems;
especially fond of hard wood seats,
not content with the one-cheek sneak,
it has to rattle off its repertoire:
fff –rrrr- rat-atat-tat !!!

Big on whis – purred – plosives –
and fond of the crisp finish:
periods and colons that signal
an explanatory clause or list
like so many geese gabbling
or ducks straining water through their bills.

Or trailing off intent in ellipses … .
Can even be interrogative – fffwha?
or imperative – poot! Or in issuance
of cartoon machine gun stammer —
like the poor kid with a speech impediment
who c-c-can't ask the girl out for a date

because he's too nervous and stutters.
Has been known to mutter on occasion –
like the kid who hides a swear word
in the fake cough he effusively
spews into his hand – a-whore! –
in the middle of a boring lecture.

Really, I ought to let him speak out
more often, instead of making him
choke on his words or clam up
in company. Let him pontificate,
interrupt the mouth once in a while,
let him let go in a good karmic/yogic sigh –

instead of squeaking like a perpetual
adolescent who's got to control
the egress of air from some rude balloon.

The mouth's so smug, after all –
What?! Because it's got control
of a few more phonemes and syllables?!

It hardly seems fair! It's not
that bad-smelling hot air never escapes
a pair of lips, is it? Or noxious
vapors never assailed a maiden's nostrils
from either orifice. Dog smells its own mess –
first smeller's the very feller, my Mom says.

Speak again, oh toothless one!
we kids would beseech, hanging
on every syllable of the anal oracle:
a corny way to cover for one of life's
little embarrassments, but it did
lend the occasions some solemnity.

An amazing muscle, really, so hep
on preserving or destroying the dignity
of man. Capable of great things –
not the least of which is distinguishing
between a solid and a gas. Unlike
any of a number of politicians I could name.

Factotum Scrotum

My wife's purple plums –
an old soldier's rucksack
for sad one-eyed Jack.

60

Conversations With My Cock

(for Sheri-D Wilson)

(1.)

Little cold wizened pizzler –
diabetes diadem asleep
on your trusty duffle bag …
Batching it again? Just diggin'
the cotton swaddlin' 'n' snugglin'
up to the warm butt
of my lady love?
Quiescent but quenched.

(2.)

Ol' helmet head. Alert as
a gopher standing at your hole –
not much as poles go
in this horizontal landscape.
Nowhere near as cute
as our dachshund when he
rears up on his hind legs and begs –
or as endearing when I roll over.

(3.)

Willy One-Eye, trouser trout …
not the cock of this or any walk,
though you've never failed me
or any of the women you've
been lucky enough to please.

Even that bout with Zoloft
failed to quell your enthusiasm,
though, Lord knows, I've
had to tug on you often enough
for the pullet surprise.

Funny tag-end of me, really.
you look like some kind
of valve wanting a wet
pair of lips – as if my ego
needs inflation, let alone
the proverbial spare tire!

(4.)

So what's with the locker room talk –
all the jeers and towel thwacks
just because you am not Sanforized [1]
there, son? A little shy of water are we?
Wee wee wee. Wanna stay warm
and engorged like some luminescent
sea pen in the briny deep,
waggin' away like an inflated
set of rubber gloves – Mickey Mouse
hands maybe? (A great gag
if you happen to be hitch hiking.)
But, hey, you rise to the occasion
and stand at attention soon enough –
and with the least provocation!
You want more damn head pats
Than my retriever, for chrissakes!
You'd think you did something
to warrant praise, or at the very least
a rubber or milk bone biscuit.
quit winkin' at me! I'm serious!

63

---

1.   From an advertisement on packaged briefs: means pre-shrunk.

(5.)

And another thing: Do you think
maybe you could let go
of that last drop of piss
before I tuck you back
into your briefs, there bro'?

I know. I know. "No matter how
you shake and dance,
the last drop goes down your pants."
I've heard it before. It's not funny!
I'm getting' old! You gonna just
sigh and let go like some kind
of cheap ballpoint in my pocket?

What?! I've gotta slap
a pinchcock on yer sorry neck?!
Honestly! You'd think you were
some runny-nosed junky
in need of a fix. I'll fix you all right!
I'll wring yer bloody neck!

(6.)

Hey! Smart guy! Glamour glans!
You're not the wife's best friend!
Don't make me laugh! You think
for one minute she wouldn't turn
her back on you if she could train
a dildo to take out the garbage?!

Oh yeah. There you go again!
Standing around tryin' to look cool
like some office exec in turtle neck
and herringbone. Gonna press your point home?
Get that secretary's back against a wall
so you can talk her ear off
over Christmas cocktails, are you?
Hey, you don't think you smell like fish?!

News flash! You're the damn nudibranch!
Think a quick swish in the sink
will make that phlegm you're regurgitating
taste any less like bleach and egg whites?
What was it Mary said? "... semen ...

scented like buckwheat honey/
a sweetness mixed with urine?" [2]
Ha! That's if they love you more
than turkey necks and giblets! [3]

(7.)

So I'm on the Atkin's diet – [4]
have lost twenty-five pounds
and can see you staring at the floor.

What's next with this diabetes nightmare,
now that my blood readings are A-O.K.?
You're not going to go south now?!

My feet are cold sometimes,
but I haven't taken to wearing
socks to bed, quite yet, there, bud!

Still, I've got to watch my extremities –
That means you too, helmet head.
Soldier on, will you – please?

---

2 Mary di Michele's lines, from her poem "Weary of Lilacs"
3 Reference to a line in Sylvia Plath's novel, The Bell Jar.
4 Dr. Robert C. Atkins, author of New Diet Revolution

I want to die in the saddle –
not one-hand reining into some
sunset on the old folks' carousel.

Chin up, chump! We've been through
a lot! Remember that lesbian nurse
who decided to humour you on a whim?

I didn't know, and you sure as hell
weren't listening! We put away
a lot of wine to get in her knickers.

Then you start sawin' a log!
No big deal. We both laughed at you then.
Just don't cop the big Z on me now, o.k.?

I'm not going to start carving my name
in the snow bank just to please you.
So forget the beady-eyed squint there, Bogie.

I'm the pissant poet, not you, o.k.?
Tell Freud to bend over and touch his toes:
I'll show him where the wild goose goes!

Ode To My Pancreas

Yo! Pancreas, old knob,
listen up! I've got an offer
I hope you can't refuse.

You start making more insulin
and I'll lay off the Twinkies –
Do we have a deal?

I know I haven't been kind.
You're working overtime
producing the damn stuff,

and all I've given you for your pains
is more carbohydrates – pies,
pizza, pasta, rice, potatoes.

I know you've been sorely taxed
trying to make enough juice
to keep me in glucose. I do!

And I've been a lazy mo' fo'
fillin' my face with pizza and beer
while you've been smokin' and stokin'.

I didn't mean to take you for granted,
and you have every right to
get pissed and pack it in –

Only if you pack 'er in,
so will my eyes, eventually,
or my dick. You know I like my dick!

It's my second favourite organ –
after you of course. And my brain maybe –
Is that an organ? Where would you be

if I couldn't walk to the refrigerator
to take out some nutritious treat –
the kind you approve of – eggs, meat?

Look! I'll make you an omelet –
every day, if necessary. And I'll
lay off the toast and jam.

Hell, I'll forgo the vanilla ice cream
(You know I love that!) and cookies!
I'll be good. No seconds, I promise!

Only don't let my dick drop off
or shrivel from a geoduck
siphon to some little neck.

There's my wife to think of,
if you can't forgive me. She
did nothing to deserve such a fate!

Whaddya say? I'll cut the carbos
to a minimum – maybe have
the odd chocolate bar or beer –

after I've walked the dogs
or jogged around the lake – every day –
only as a reward, mind you!

You start producing more or get
the other organs to pump the juice
through my sorry ass pipes

and I'll pump iron! Come on!
Don't be such a squished banana!
I'm not getting enough sex as it is!

I'm sufferin', baby! You've taught me
to be more considerate. Give me a break!
I can still get it up and think straight.

I've got glasses now; my toes are cold.
Isn't that punishment enough? I'm only
fifty for chrissakes! I'm goin' bald!

Have a heart! How would you feel
if all your islets started drifting apart?
We're a community here. You, me –

What?! Do you want me to beg?
O.K., I'm on my knees … Pretty please?!
Pretty please with a cherry on top?!

The Islets of Langerhans

*(with apologies to W.B. Yeats,
and for fellow sufferer, Rienzi Crusz)*

I will arise and go now
with fellow carbohydrate junkies
whose overworked pancreases cry ow!
Uncle already! With mice and monkeys

to the fabled Islets of Langerhans
in tropic seas, where coconut palms
and warm stretches of white sands
allow me to warm my tootsies, sing psalms.

And I will repent of the many chocolate bars
and sundry junk food treats I did consume
beneath gibbous moons and twinkling stars
in cooler climes, while lonely in my room.

And I will get up off my butt –
stop stuffing myself with munchies –
tubing before the one-eyed monster to get my glut
of alpha-loboto waves and crunchies.

Only, please, Lord, no more eights,
or – worse – fourteens on my Accu-Soft
glucose meter! I'll lift weights,
abstain from sweets! Hold my head aloft

though it wobble under the weight
of so many inane bites of infoflab
and bafflegab! No seconds on my plate,
babe! For ever and ever, while I nab

a nap. And pray to St. Insulin
to lose my belly if not all the excess weight
and shut off the telly and sin
some other way, while Peter holds the gate.

Talking Back To Zoloft

How can you and I be friends?
Our relationship is ambivalent at best.
I spend quality time with you – every day –
at my wife's urging, and in truth,
you do help, do level out my moods.

You're cute too in your little fifty
mg, yellow and white bomber jacket,
and you take the curves en-route
to your destination with grace and elan,
never squeal your tires or lose the road.

You're expensive though and I
don't like to line the body men's and mechanics'
pockets, even if I can write you off
and get reimbursed for your
shenanigans and escapades.

And, make no mistake, you're
a fair weather friend, if that.
Sure, it's fun to motor along with you –
to take those crazy curves
at a hundred miles an hour.

I like the wind in my hair – I do.
And there's still enough of it that I
can affect a leonine mane and demeanor,
but my growl was always worse
than my bite and I don't need you –

not really. Others speak your praises –
my wife especially. Are you two lovers?
Are you just taking me for a ride,
ingratiating yourself before me in the mornings
after a wicked night between my sheets?

You don't help me much in that department.
Oh , I can get it up with you –
you're sexy enough and can taunt and tease
me into a frenzy. Oh yeah, and you
keep me hard and I want to be with you.

You even make it easier for my wife
and I to fall into each others arms,
and we still make passionate love –
I won't let you insinuate yourself
between our sheets – not completely.

After being with you for a time though,
I just can't come when we're entwined.
Oh, she lets me take her from behind,
gives me head, jumps on my bones
and gyrates until our loins are afroth with foam

and I love being able to move my hips
in this frenzied dance as long as you let me.
It's great not to fire a salvo in pre-ignition
or have to storm the gates with a wet noodle.
You don't dampen my libido or enthusiasm.

But when I do hit the big O, it's not
like I hit any bell with a sledge:
it almost hurts and I don't get
the big crescendo or spontaneously say
Here we go! Before we fly off the cliff together.

It's a release and a relief to know
all systems are go when that particular
piston fires and thrusts me deep inside her
on the down stroke. And I can certainly
make her engine purr. And I do.

You have other quirks I'm not fond of too.
You make me clammy. My forehead is
always breaking out in a dew and I
have to mop you from my brow in ways
that make me look guilty of something –

or nervous when I'm in front of a class
or reading. I'm not nervous and I don't
like that. Sometimes you make me dizzy
and sweat profusely. It's not just the extra
baggage I'm carrying on a forty-four frame.

And as for my stools, you either
make me loose as a toothpaste tube
or issueth hard nuggets begrudgingly.
There doesn't seem to be any pleasing you.
You're a high maintenance bitch sometimes.

So how can you and I be friends?
My highs just aren't as high without
the lows. When we're together I don't get
so angry, true, and I am able to live
with your outbursts too. We're just not simpatico.

Do I get in the little fifty mg with you,
careen around every street with my
thinning hair streaming, a smile on my face?
Or do I banish you to the outer Hebrides
of my soul and hone my anger to a blade?

It's a tough call and tough duty
riding with you. I get scared. My
butt cheeks want to pull cotton
right out of the seat sometimes.
I don't know where you're taking me.

Little serotonin re-uptake inhibitor,
you keep my molecules humming
and I love the way you make my engine purr,
but I don't want my cylinders re-bored,
I don't want to be chopped and modified.

I'm a four-banger at heart. Dependable,
if not always reliable. And when I fly
off the proverbial handle looking for
a misplaced pen or correcting misplaced
modifiers, I at least own my emotions.

Others may want to disown me at times,
and I admit, without you, I am no one's
cup of tea or long cool drink of water.
I'm a little Napoleon who wants to pull
his bone apart. Always horny, frequently irate.

I'm a little volcano, a magma pool
of seething hates and grumbles. I erupt,
I spew, I froth and bubble and pop.
I leave a bad smell in a room after
I've erupted. My wife sometimes hates me.

So, my fine weather friend, what do we do?
Fuck each other senseless? Re-tool my genes
hot grooves? Re-gap my spark plugs?
Let you consume my dendrites in a brush fire
until I'm calm and have no fuel to burn?

You're an insidious little molecule
and I don't know whether you'll be
the death of me or I'll be the death of you.
Just don't get uppity with your glib talk
of designer genes, increased energy and joy, O.K.?

If we have this little chat now and again
and I talk of throwing you over for that
other daemon or muse, and anger turns
its blade to my own heart and mind,
you'll understand: we're not friends.

You may not be Mother's Little Helper.
You might not wheedle and cajole
to have your way with me. You might not
even be able to seduce me with your
velvet voice and sultry, sexy ways,

but you don't have to. I'll ride along
with you for a while – maybe longer.
I'll love my wife, make peace with
my other demons if need be. But
I'm not about to crown you queen for a day.

My muse doesn't run on high octane fuel.
She doesn't have high cheek bones
and 3500 p.s.i. pneumatic lips or
blade like hips. Her ass certainly can't
pull nails out of the wall,

but she makes my little fireman's hat
glow red, and when I enter the burning house
with her, the conflagration that consumes us
burns with an even glow and my synapses
crackle and send sparks aloft. Oh, they do!

So do me a favor, Zelda baby.
Don't get all up in my body the way you do.
Take a back seat once in a while. Don't grab
at my staff of life and blow the walls apart
when you blow me. Don't shake my fever tree.

Don't go down on me when I'm driving either.
I mean, I like it – I do – but it makes it
hard to control the car, and I like
who I'm becoming. I really do. That's not
a boast or idle braggadocio either.

Let Pinnochio's nose grow and sniff out
what it came here for. Roses certainly, the
particular piquancy of my real muse.
I've gotten used to her. I know her kinks.
We have a lifetime to iron out the wrinkles.

81

Boy in a Red Shirt on a Trampoline

The little boy on the trampoline
tries so earnestly to please:
up, down, higher and higher,
as if, in reaching the still point
between the ascent and the descent,
he could slow the rhythm of his heart's
own tympanic beat to the elastic
rhythm of his breathing, the soft
slow sproing of his stocking feet
against and in the very weave
of the exact center of the trampoline.

See how he brings his legs together,
how he point his toes just so,
legs slightly apart when he alights,
arms like bird wings in the bath,
shaking off the last drops of sunlight
from his splayed fingertips –
a phoenix of ambition arising
from the ash of his own gracelessness
to say "Look! Look at me!",

sweat flying like welding sparks
from his forehead and his hair.

But there are no spotters now
his mother and father, who would
break his every fall and prevent him
from catapulting past the perimeter
of the springs and sky-blue frame
of this last perfect summer day,
are bouncing to a slacker weave
in a different city, a different season
half a continent away. And still,
the child in him jumps, jumps
up, down, higher and higher
while the sun leaks like orange pekoe
through the tight weave of the backyard fence.

He does a perfect forward somersault now,
arms clapped to his side, knees tucked up
and tight into his abdomen, chin to chest —
while over his right shoulder the foetal moon
rolls listlessly in its own amniotic heaven.

Up, down, higher and higher
he would jump for you,
now arching his back,
arms stretched out in a perfect
crucifix, feet inscribing the sky
in a backwards somersault –
head at six, feet at twelve –
his smile a perfect excision in time.

Right now he wishes his body could
align itself perfectly with yours,
to determine once and forever
the precise azimuth of desire.
He wants desperately and always
to land on his feet,
to please the man with
the salt and pepper beard,
looking out a back window,
steaming ceramic mug in hand,
about to taste the sunset at his lips.

III

A Dule of Doves

Whimpering in his
golden retriever sleep,
jowls quivering,
his feet twitch, chest heaves,
but which shore does he reach?

•

from the grey brain
of the hefty wasp hive
one vector of thought

•

all the flags are limp,
but the zucchinis
are engorged with light

•

weeping birch branches
flounce in an August squall—
I miss the yield sign

•

cabbage whites flutter
among zucchini blossoms —
her hand on my thigh

•

So many weeds!
I don't wonder that any
half holy man could
walk across these still waters
in a pair of rubber thongs.

•

cloudy, but still warm ...
I watch the first stars'
slow striptease

•

lavendar sky —
forest fire smoke
turns the moon red

•

At your father's grave
our son asks for the name of
hanging Spanish Moss —
I recall the less common
moniker of Old Man's Beard

•

enough light to see
but too many mosquitoes
to hold the pencil!

•

"Please keep to the walks,"
decorative green signs say —
grass tuft in asphalt
(Nikka Yuko Japanese Garden)

•

No koi?!
Birds shit on the stones
the guide demurs
(Nikka Yuko Japanese Garden)

•

whirlygig beetle
grabs a bubble
for a diving bell

•

flying tandem
dragonflies in heat
touch the pond's surface —
like Tinkerbell's wand
the little girl offers

•

her death so sudden –
hummingbird sips nectar
as you cup the phone
(for Dave and Louella)

•

to kill or not to —
the wasp nest its own
paper brain

•

one sharp yelp –
still dachshund pup snaps
at the grounded wasp

•

at your father's grave
Spanish moss-covered oaks –
I remember his
beard changed colour after
the chemotherapy
(for Gepke)

•

so humid, so still –
two ants struggle with
a dead house fly

•

chipmunk's cheeks full
of peanuts and trail mix –
the shadows lengthen

•

bumblebee bumbles
in a bergamot blossom –
gong note longer now
(Nikka Yuko Japanese Garden)

•

cool today – at last!
even ants on the sidewalk
walk slowly

•

branch almost fully
turbanned by the wasp nest–
one apple protrudes

•

blue light through the trees –
distant campfire beckoning?
no, big screen t.v.

•

finally, no wind!
a cottonwood seed descends
paratrooper style

•

windfall apples –
tiny dachshund chew toys
with green fuse stems

•

as the neighbour's saw
rips, screams through
another board,
first yellow leaf falls

• • •

Victoria Flower & Garden Show, Royal Roads 2003

Pricey admission!
Thirty-two bucks to see
insect porn!

•

In the middle of
the flower and garden show,
the beer garden!

•

colonial style —
driftwood arms, rope seat:
two hundred bucks!

•

At the flower show
attendants subtly arrange
parking lot cars!

•

after so many
gardening vendor pitches
wanting to walk to
the breakwater
to look for purple starfish

• • •

so much depends on
cheaply made red wheelbarrow
88694

•

muggy afternoon —
cop sets up his speed trap
and smirks

•

voices, car door slam —
between my feet
dachshund harrumphs

•

reading haiku —
a tiny red mite
traverses a page

•

big kerfuffle
over Scatalogue art show —
dog shits question mark

•

mute birds
on the power lines
compose sheet music

•

jeweler's not open —
I need a watch battery
of course

•

end of summer —
smell of forest fire smoke
in the lumber yard

•

first spring walk —
retriever pees on
each and every tree

•

cottonwood seed drifts —
fly approaches, hovers
for a closer look

•

first rain of the year!
first time I've dashed into it
to smell the sidewalk

Acknowledgements

Some of the poems in this collection have previously appeared in the following journals and e-zines: *Event, Moments, The Nashwaak Review, Nightingale, Rags, Regina Weese, Signal Magazine, Simply Haiku, Waterblossoms, West End Writer's Club* ("Guest Spot" page), *The Windsor Review*. Several appeared in the following anthologies and web collections: *Body Language: a Head to Toe Anthology,* edited by John B. Lee (Black Moss Press, 2003); *Idling: Excursions Into Unemployment,* edited by Lee O'Tolstoy (Bob Wakulich); *I Want To Be The Poet of Your Kneecaps: Poems of Quirky Romance,* edited by John B. Lee (Black Moss Press, 1999); *Losers First: Poems and Stories on Game and Sport,* edited by John B. Lee (Black Moss Press, 1999), *North By North Wit: An Anthology of Canadian Humour,* Edited by Dale Jacobs (Black Moss Press, 2003)

A handful appeared in the "new poems" section of my earlier book, *A Murder of Crows: New & Selected Poems* (Black Moss Press, 1998) and in *Wiser Pills* (HMS Press Books on Disc, 1995). I reproduce them here because of their thematic connection to this text. Thanks to all the editors concerned for their interest and support of my work, and to the editors of magazines and journals not mentioned who first published some of the poems that subsequently appeared in *Wiser Pills* and *A Murder of Crows*. I am grateful to you all.

I: UNEMPLOYED IN SHANGRI-LA

II: BODY ENGLISH

III: A DULE OF DOVES

ACKNOWLEDGEMENTS